&luckier

The Mountain West Poetry Series
Stephanie G'Schwind & Donald Revell, series editors

&luckier

poems

Christopher J Johnson

The Center for Literary Publishing
Colorado State University

For information about permission to reproduce
selections from this book, write to
The Center for Literary Publishing
attn: Permissions
9105 Campus Delivery, Colorado State University
Fort Collins, Colorado 80523-9105.

Printed in the United States of America.

Library of Congress Cataloging-in-Publication Data

Names: Johnson, Christopher J (Christopher Jamie), 1981- author.
Title: &luckier : poems / Christopher J Johnson.
Other titles: And luckier | Mountain west poetry series.
Description: Fort Collins, Colorado : Center for Literary Publishing,
    Colorado State University, 2016. | Series: The mountain west poetry series
Identifiers: LCCN 2016032837 (print) | LCCN 2016035240 (ebook) | ISBN
    9781885635518 (pbk. : alk. paper) | ISBN 9781885635525 (electronic)
Classification: LCC PS3610.O32397 A6 2016 (print) | LCC PS3610.O32397
(ebook)
    | DDC 811/.6--dc23

2016032837

The paper used in this book meets the minimum requirements of the American
National Standard for Information Sciences-Permanence of Paper for Printed
Library Materials, ANSI Z39.48-1984.

1 2 3 4 5   20 19 18 17 16

ACKNOWLEDGMENTS

I would like to thank all of my teachers; they have been everyone and have come
from everywhere and, more often than not, put up with my unending questions. In
particular Dana Levin. Also, the *American Poetry Review* and *West Branch Wired*
for first publishing some of these poems.

for the depths of Vostok & Jupiter's ancient storm — for all curious things.
&for the faces we make when we don't know what faces we should make.

&for my mom &my sister &my dad.

And to die is different from what any one supposed, and luckier.

—Walt Whitman, *Song of Myself*

CONTENTS

Lifestones

Local Transits

Atolls

Local Transits II

LIFESTONES

We have forgot our gods

We have forgot our gods. They sleep in us;
hoar-frost, the crocodile ### his tooth& oaks,
figs in fig trees& fig wasps fucking in their depths,
thunderbolts, all sleep in us as gods.

There are plastic petals for winter& fall visitors
but i cannot live alone thru man's riles& rigor,
      the industries of his hands& fingers;

i am indebted to the sparrow, nasturtiums,
nettles& pollen grain, i am indebted to each season,
      inert sand& the weather's whim.

i came here thru the same table as the cockroach
&couldn't have w/out his persistence.

Bach could hear the crickets

Bach could hear the crickets
in their slow sets,
their music of the spheres
spilling skyward from the grass
&Sundays he'd leak it into his neighbors' breasts;

i've seen unbearable grief in the eyes of cats,
having learned to read eyes like arrivals& departures,
having learned them like airplanes
— savage contradictions: seared with loving,
proud with pain, lit with hope thru knowing defeat —

i am some every —
. . . i don't know what —
i am some all like air& dark matter,
. . . quasar& dirt;

the dead i sow into myself,
for the dead i bless the rocks.

Do we pulse so strange

Do we pulse so strange?
More abstract than the cracked glass of winter elms,
more erratic than the breathing of this unconscious bird
                         so small in my palm;
are we more intricate, more in-depth,
are our ways less applicable to death
than the oyster who is silent& never slanders?
Than pressuring fathoms are we more vast?
Than wild gardens, more numerous?
&against the lightward vine do we have
                  more craft, more genius
or judging before we act do we have greater judgment
than the lynx who is swift& accurate?
is our precious substance to arrange the fork
or cure the flesh, cheat at cards or lose interest,
         to stumble& fail to explain ourselves?

It occurred to me

It occurred to me life was something we wanted
even deep in our wounds ###
though it fall to something like the nothing
before& after a serenade;
we bring it roses& names, give it deity,
&always say — are always saying —
                         — we give word
&parcel it in metaphor, ourselves just bits
of the whole where we lay our awe &odes
                — black box of our travels.

Our kindnesses& dourness, all of our faces
will wash from the page. We will return
like ribs to a ribcage.

I am unlike nothing

I never had a need for wine in my water jug.
Against all improbability i yawned
&danced &walked my little map.

&i was wrong to ask what i am
rather than what am i different from,
sharing with space its startling depth
&with the alligator, his smile& tooth
&with the bark of trees, coarseness;

&i wear them in the deep pattern of my organs
in written words that are older than voices,
in the unceasing chatter of my form;

with the bark i share bitterness,
with water i share sustenance;

i regard everything, i give it a name;

i am unlike nothing.

Somewhere beneath this dirt

Somewhere beneath this dirt
   the seeds are tomorrow —
or choking; i don't know.

&, really, i find it all so erased —
         what I've done,

i mean who i was
      comes& goes
&, sometimes, works out different
       than what i remember.

It's gotten cold.
Not every tree, not every limb
       will return.
Familiar clothes are tossed down our arms
&what could not is broken down
       to restore ourselves
       &smokes thru the woods —
i know this better than i know myself;

     everywhere, always
       i am returning —
   i don't know how
     &i am not return-
        ing also.

p.s.

  I am not return-
ing; i won't leave.
  as i am, i am

stamped in everything, the
        bends of my sleeves —
        i will not leave . . .

The miles i stamped
        w/ my heels, the miles
i traced in thought& need
  are mine, are mine only
  &they are always.

And we ought to consider

&we ought to consider how we go on,
how we lace& unlace the shoe —
how we resole& how, eventually, replace it whole;
we ought to consider how the skin sheds& grows
&the bones build, the bones break& build& hollow
&nothing remains of our births but,
we ought to consider the structure of our peripheral;
what we see is not but we deem
&what we love is not yet seems to be,
what we love is not but changes always
&grows& shrinks& barbs or evaporates;

&the words sd. are the words as a corpse
&the words sd. are a string which frays
&the single word is a bead rolled beneath
&the words spoke are a broken clasp
&yet we ought to consider how we go forth.

All these gods that leak into the muscles

All these gods that leak into the muscles,
that lather us in their cloudbursts,
we are their priests, their temples,
a canvas stretched to the purpose of their use;

theirs is a constant breadth, centerless,
that slides from face to face,
concealing or baring teeth;

we're stock clips of their image:
flinch, clench, blushing or otherwise red,
folding in to our own flesh
as if to jamb into a suitcase or umbrella stand,
straightening our stance, crying out in ready action,
sad, ecstatic or inert, bland;

our emotions have us,
we're golems of their whim
&they stamp themselves on our foreheads.

The earth, the mountains move

The earth, the mountains move,
they calm& rush like oceans
everything is building& sloughing;
if we could hear all time
tinctured into this moment,
it would not sing. time would scream.

there is a moment that coaxed the birds to flight,
in which the antelopes learned the grace of their legs
&borealis bloomed like a bruise on the sky's face
&i, too, from this lineage;

i was exiled from god
when I first thought on myself
&what i was.

What else?

We sleep& wake in the bottleneck of it,
always in the richest — heavy or light — moment;
i'm glad to spend it by myself or
within my dozens, pressing forth with hundreds.

&i don't run from the blossoming of my blood
or shy back from the thunder in my head
&i don't stand afraid when the horizon is wide
around me alone.

the sky is my kin, i understand his storm;
distance my cousin,
understanding a want for separateness
despite the impossibility of it;
all of us, everything; what else?

What words there are

What words there are, who can say?
What is said evaporates, freezes, or feeds;
words spoken never keep their forms,
suiting themselves to ears& evidence.

Nothing assimilates& comes out sane.

Days wreck in us, a confused lore of ships,
specters& retired currency.

The light eats up half of us
as we walk away from any point,
the rest go blind looking back.

Yet our dust will rise& sing,
be green, &star, &flesh
thru many systems.
Our dust will find harmony in bonds
as rigid as calm.

But all in all

But all in all, all from that first breath,
Erato, Clio, Calliope joined at the hips
&of a single lineage w/ voice variants
&the beetle has as many epics
&the sparrow his lyric richness
&both &more have left their hieroglyphs
       — all have come thru this sole passage,
the ape, the man& oak, the dormouse each at their oars
&so many more have cleft those waves before
       &still cleft thru our soil& arms;
in pop, in Paleolithic song sung by chance& time;
not sand inert or dust will miss fire& pulse
nor fail to sprout& leaf
&all will collapse& rise again in the steam
&grow firm thru gentleness, thru rain,
hurtling forth from the damp-footed forest,
drift& morph in islands& chains —
even as avenues stretch& shrink
&wear away or inlay the fields& deserts,
eke out the ocean cliffs, homes bob& drift
on the ocean's lips — follow tides, they skiff,
or hitch by trucks, these are fractions short& lasting
as migration outlives species' cunning v's,
       a rhythm on passing wings,
as we in our immortal resurfacing
do kiss& shift interiors, shift photos in their permanent frames,
gather in or let the skirts hang, grow& crop the hair.

What if what is to be has passed

What if what is to be has passed
&our consciousness is a deceit that arrests us?
What if thought were the consciences of fate
                    expiated on our frames?

What if the fingernail-scale purple asters
were already smeared across our summers' hills;
the lithe fish in their clear streams — pan& bones;
the finite trees proliferated, subspeciesed& deceased;
what if we're as ghosts who yearn for souls,
reflect somberly& scheme against our bodies
                    as against crashed planes?

What if our words are already stabbed& stumbled
or don't exist w/ the weight we think they have
&all are Sundays are spent, already, in sweat& white

&what if each oar stroke were a solid gesture,
a suggestion of a whir upon seas still as parking lots,
the moon run its influence, sunk into the sun's death;
this moment's shadows already sunk beneath themselves
&stretched& in the dusk dissolved?

I am not a plotter of would'ves

I am not a plotter of would'ves
always forgetting what i've said to myself
&, after all, there is only now&,
possibly, some days after.

I'm not sure what the significance of today is,
i mean, i know its name,
nocturnal& diurnal allowance; still,
i'm not sure why i track this,
today is just where i am.

Today i made a dollar, ate well& slept,
&performed the rituals of my flesh
w/soap, i shaved;

When i bare my teeth, when i am just intuition,
what my animal tells me i can't say,
though i know you know&
are dumb as well.

I lay in the sun, prostrate, stretched upon a rock;
time tore thru me, matter, space& change
&i lost my form, as i am always losing it,
rising& leaving myself;

&i felt sadness for the stones
which, they say, are motionless;
nothing is, not even Styrofoam nor
dead trucks; i'm no plotter of would haves,
i'm never satisfied with schemes (which
are toward ideals); first, i notice it, then
i admire the weather . . .

Where are the dead

Where are the dead?
How shall we make mention of them?
Are they in the weeds& trees
or some heaven of our heads,
                    both,
or do they pace the scaffolds of our world?

Where do they sit& sip things?
Where do they sigh& smother themselves in arms?

How shall we mention them?
Always restricted to past tense
            &good& right
or shall we give them our face
to use as they wish
give them the body slump or cautious
or rolling back into sleep;
shall we give them our bodies,
our new days like tools?

&who are they anyway?
Do they never change or change
only in our minds? Are they me?
How can they rest so differently
in the labyrinths of our many throats& brains?

        I don't know.

But we aren't just monsoons,
downpours& fierce winds, seasons,
                    but tributary systems;
we are the arch of time& word
&where i go, they will come too,

&what i say, they've said also,
&how they've smiled is in my smile,
&when i've gone, i'll be with you.

The moth floundered

The moth floundered in the warm dust
while the black widow boxed the locust,
there was caution in the crow's movements,
new shoots thru cement
&fragments of their freedom in my pant cuffs —

between me& all this is only nothing
&an infinite distance, my view& many cold disinterests.
Between the blank moon& the moon filled,
thru its growth is my lean, slight shadow, clothes
&my hands in their moods,
between plans& the animal i am, only conception;

&my hands are very sure things
they work w/ a grace beyond me
to wrangle like hawks out of free fall
some object of instinctual longing,
they have the surety of saints in their azure veins.

There is nothing i could return to this,
to all of it but its very clearness
such as delights the feeble-minded
or very young children; there is separation in nothing
but the minds of men.

The ruined wall

The ruined wall   the stone table
overlook river flow
        from the north (my right).
Don't ask *where are they now*
though their hands
were fluid as birds
        about this masonwork;
threefold: foundation, home, ruin.

Our eyes cannot compass time,
all succulence, all fullness at once
builders moved thru this growth, their sons
&all their concerns& further back
the oar strokes thick as earth
&, further,
        the ground too chill to break . . .

But all returns to our blood,
there are none
who don't sing in us now
        more thick than iceflow.

Their passage is deeper than the hour,
it's bracken round these stones
&the dust that flows from their friction,
                seamless in all things,
sustenance for the next question.

LOCAL TRANSITS

Self Portrait

Some frail sticks is all
&sinuous mud to cake them in,
with an extra volume
to keep me from snapping in the wind,

but what wonder this strange ruin
where what i am is what dwells between
&though i wear away& break& mend
i am ever the same
like the warmth in a deep deep cave.

I am not sure if I am no one

I am not sure if i am no one or many many men
or myself or a fragment dreamed —
i am not sure if i am homo sapiens sapiens,
if i am of myth& ocean, math or all these
i am uncertain, perhaps mixtures
or a Rubik's Cube of ancestral gesture:
the curl of my lip theirs, the roots of my bicuspids
&small startled exhalations, the smoke of my longing eyes
&the creases that'll come w/ age;
i am not certain if the words& voices mean anything
&still i gargle them& shoot from my hand
&pin them to an image
&still i abstain& i cannot.

Having thumbs

Having thumbs& they opposable
&my tongue w/ its eloquent volume —
i can hold nothing incontrovertibly
nor fast w/ any sleight of speech,
nothing, i mean, fits in my bag.

My brother-in-law w/ his cunning weight,
his dog w/ its swift weight& the weight
of my sister thru the growth of her life,
my beloved's weight tucked into mine
        &the weight of my Wednesdays
          of my Saturday mornings
&of the golden leaf caught in my throat;
nothing hangs right from my shoulders.

When i am transmuted into coin,
i mean, a silver in coup w/ my being,
when my friends hold their hats if hats are in,
i mean, when everyone agrees they knew me;
            i'll fit in a box, perfectly.

Because everything

Because everything, everything is an addition;
nothing is a failure& growing old
       is merely a swelling the cup,
            a sipping of life
                 progress.

&don't repent; everything becomes us:
every misstep, twig, our guilt, our breath,
       as when the bones snap
        they marrow back more thick.
Don't repent, don't choose a chaplain
when you've regiments. Nobility has several forms
&is not always calm& can have so many questions.

I have sat upon café walls

I have sat upon café walls
little but stickish bones, a scarecrow
puffed-up w/ rags, smoking at the mouth
&i have made a machine of myself
that took to emotions as do metal slabs;

i've sat inside me& watched the world, like montage, pass
or've idolized moments past
&cast expectations curse on future events;
i've lost hours& hours at hand to all forms of rest;

in a instant i've gathered up myself& stepped into an ocean current,
&i've stood atop a very very high place
&thought of aether& Augustine, Da Vinci's flying machines;

i've recessed into pills, for months sleeping . . .

i have nearly dissolved in the shock of a breeze
&i've let my thoughts stray w/ their own seriousness,
have let my thoughts feel contempt for my flesh
&'ve blushed w/ the shame of it.

And what more can I give

And what more can i give,
having given the softness of my hands
&the arrow of my spine,
having given the word of what i've suffered,
what more can i give them?

i've seen us hold in whatever
we wouldn't take home
as if it were a stone in our ribs
pushing our bellies to our knees
i have felt it, what is inconsolable;

the ash of our ancestors
which we wear like sad notices,
like evictions, or place in ourselves
as if we were pockets for incinerated coin;
&all for words so simple you could laugh at them,
words like car, water, necktie, words like shelter.

What a lush world

What a lush world it is: preparing for events
&exonerating one's self w/ friends
&so many communiqués&
the stamp up, the public transit;
how shall i sit to the right& to the left of me;
                    how shall I behave?

Summer's in with its southern wind
&everyone gets strange, the days don't end;
porches are nocturnal terrariums
&voices carry like knives thru the evening.

We're all jack-o-lanterns;
terrifying, fragile faces,
brief small flames&
            all in the head.

Having shut the door on my extended facts

Having shut the door on my extended facts,
turned my key& told myself that life, this life,
is the tune that sounds thru my instrument;
saying, so often i have aired the ways of a man:
gesturing w/ umbrella, man in brown coat;
man descends a staircase
in a tie w/ cigarette; often, man on park bench;
man w/ black socks looks into mail box . . .

&i am aware, then, of a certain texture
woven thru time: man in yellow jacket;
man offering arm; crook of an old man . . .

I am aware of a weave my habits have
&see it worn also on men who rise early to read,
beyond the variations that pass thru their hands:

inquisitive man regards a cello stand;
man in red hat holds a box shape;
man in olive pants lights a match;
hunched man, w/ downcast glance, holds a black hat:
formally attired man claps amidst seated audience;
man in mourning dress presses face into his sleeve;
man in bathrobe dancing . . .

I've hollowed out these lines

I've hollowed out these lines, this voice
so you may fit& you& you,
because i couldn't stand alone, i never
                              wanted to.

Listen, nobody's up there,
how much noise would that make,
all those sandals, cleats, &bare feet;
so i've made you, here, a little space to fit

&i tell you this,
there is so much in yr face
that i never thought of going anywhere else.

And with these tools

And with these tools we will yet construct
so many fine ships& set them fast
to sail them out towards those unknown to us.

There is no will in it, who we *become*
whether we are standing in line
assuming the postures of strangers
or matching our voice to theirs,
or if it's faces worn into our flesh
with love& time, phrases
that form exclusive languages;

of what is familiar we leave so little
&whether we go forward or below
we aren't alone, we aren't hardly ourselves.

* * * * * * * * * * * * * * * * *

The tokens, i think, don't mean anything
— Roman coins, effigies, prayers,
but i'm certain of a vault in me,
some depth where everything still exists:

                          every fraction
&refraction of the moon, every laugh,
each cough, every sobbing contraction
&when we go we don't go far, but, often, i know
when the way will be less kind.

It is so. The devil . . .

It is so. The devil comes thru the noon sun
w/ an off-word or passing gorgeous in a black Saab,
&it takes nothing, you shall know him,
rising in the blood or as a clump at the back of yr throat,
even hidden, thoroughly white, in the clench of a fist,
or cold cold tact behind a calm sentence,
in the blindness of an open eye's film, a seal for sounds,
&stabbing guts thru the very tips of his toes
&i have heard him sly in a jealous mouth,
&in such a way felt him pass thru myself,
detached w/ a dreadful ambivalence,
&he's a fire upon a man, his accounts, his belly, lips
the devil is a fire of thirst;
&though he shiver thru the air which surrounds defeat
he is man-shape most.

I have kept, today, to myself

I have kept, today, to myself,
having dropped a stone on my politics.
in pondering the escargot of scent
from the autumn trees folding in their bereavements,
i have dropped a stone on this.

&today, as i leaf thru my poet,
i sense an aphid in my foliage,
the diminished hunger of my full-animal,
my attendance fall away from its pews,
my fondest ghosts fold into daylight&
my feminine tuck into herself;
i have lost faith in my number;
somewhere in my NATO regiments disagree
&fall away from themselves;

today, i can see my breath expiate for my death
in the trees that sprout from my mouth,
i drop a stone on this.

I know my death

I know my death, i authored it
though, still, to go on two legs
&hold it in while i use the spoon
&wonder what the weather will be
                when i am sleeping . . .

What's a soul for, i can't master its use;
it damages my mouth& fails so in my groin.
How's it strange, always longing
so that i cannot be alone,
is it incomplete, malformed?

        — to communicate, to talk
        is to press against rock
        &imagine you swim thru it.

Let's not bake bricks

Let's not bake bricks in our thoughts' ovens
nor burn ourselves w/ fires of retrospect,
my ear is an ampoule for sadness;
i make a magic circle of a certain depth
&have an eye to praise light in the dark places;

i've been thru the public of dagger tips,
the thick ponk of brutal voices —
absorbed the blows of those mortally wounded
by lost stones cast into their memory's cruelness
&'ve exhausted the groaning fist,
lulled it to sleep on my patient flesh;

&braver still in the hospitals.
i've uttered the secret words (no wards themselves),
have sd., "gumdrop" "dowry" "Stevens"
&'ve been inspected for zippers,
have read the tortures scrawled on green boards:

Laura, BITCH, exquisite corpse, Osiris, whore
&the suits of cards.

This is my smiling face, my wolfish, this my serious,
my sleep face, vicious& this my anguish . . .

DON'T FORGET:

i pull faces from yr face's deck.

I would rather somewhere I never

Some days i am all weight& cannot start
something uncivil in my inner ear
argues what i will or won't.

Epiphany is a selfish ecstasy,
realizing for oneself what has fallen out;

i would rather somewhere i never,
strangers' faces are more understandable.
Wherever i am, i'm among friends
&, today, that's all wall;

it doesn't make sense,
some days one only cares about planets
on others: taxes, dinner plans, the Page of Wands
(bartenders don't polish glasses to make them clean,
they polish them to pass time).

I am dark for —

I am dark for —
        i do not know
— this is not to be released from the throat —
    the voice, a tool to distrust;
having seen yr words chide yr looks
having seen you rigid at a false "yes."

        &i am dark for — not this alone,
but the cinema of time, that seems to unfold
thru choice& circumstance, but is all cut,
produced& placed, each frame, in a finished film:

                the tide does not come in
                the sun is& isn't
                colors emerge& are forgotten
                giants rotate in their chains& locks — everything
                has an anchor in its meaning.

I don't choose, i keep my course
however often i rise& argue w/ myself
                — though i struggle to change;

i'm dark for —
        being all brick,
blind in my usefulness
never truly knowing my shape
                or what's next, though it's
                done — already said.

Even though I have done my best

Even though i have done my best
to take account of my numbers& shapes
&even cut this infinite total back
finding it adequate to live my life thru finer selves
even though all this, still i've failed.

After all there are so many stones immovable
that fall thru the fluid of our joy
&by their oppressive weight
overflow its volume when they sink.

'Cause really nothing beats rock
but time& spring& friends,
enough sunlight, enough drink;
only rivers& oceans smooth stones.

ATOLLS

This morning in my posture's stick

This morning in my posture's stick i feel a loneliness
thru the girth of my roots;
my stone has stopped flowing, my saint is sleeping,
i feel the hair that came& went from me&
when i reach back, i wonder if the hands i greet are dead.

&this morning, from this table,
as i sit in my sagacious selves, my centipede of flesh
(in time transfixed),
as i sit in my smear of hats, at bouquets of pen
&recline in my joys& grievances, my range of smiles —
i mean to say, as i cook in my spiritual hash
i am very aware of my hands
&that the star itself has no distance.

&this afternoon, while i am walking or shifting keys,
a man will skitter to this table, coil upon the chair
&although i do not know him we form one pattern.

Ode to Ghosts (7th cranial muscle)

The homeless men drown sugar for breakfast,
they ask everything of everyone rising from dream;
&how, i've asked, do we finish successfully,
all external facts arranged,
the concertos twined in file upon the bare table
&nothing in the cupboards or fruit bowl;

i would sleep in the girth of Bach,
his organ hammers, a dulled lullaby of fugues;
none of Uriel's bass& drums have more of god's tones;

we'll sleep in the marrow of the apple's flavor,
as flightless birds are the savor of Mauritian sugar,
we'll sleep in the keys played thru each instrument of face,
be haunts on the seventh;
ghosts across the cranial twitch;
consternations of muscled flesh.

Icebergs

I leave marbles on windowsills
'til they're warm w/ sun as earlobes,
then cool them in my palms
&when this is done i reflect on
how the hair's tide is very long
afore it's cropped quickly back again.
&hoard foreign buttons in brass boxes
alongside orphaned cuff links& plastic rings;

i find these such useful ways of sleeping
&do very heavily these light things.

&if all this fails i think how, if measured in length,
icebergs more than i make the saddest tears leaked.

I don't understand how the father

I don't understand how the father
whose girl is dead
can take his shoes to be resoled,
how, for him, there is more road.

&, i think for all his faults,
assuming he has faults,
he must be very strong.

Often, when i've misspoken
— i mean broached the wrong thing —
i've suffered myself very long,
scratching at my decision.

I am told, &have observed,
that fathers never find them ugly
or at odds or, even, silly
— their daughters — though they are human
&so, a million million.

&i wonder at my strengths
— if i even know them
&how i go about my tasks
with an ease lacking gravity;
how i wash& do not feel
my every hair heavy with grief.

You might think it were made by the blackbirds

You might think it were made by the blackbirds
or that they plucked it from trees
the way they dropped it on Jerome& Anthony.
If it were scarce, lines of families would shuck steam
in the cold streets, in tenements
for portions to break into fives or fours, threes,
as if it were aseptic, to be relished,

a twin to breath, though opposite in substance.

It's a field wrecked& condensed into scrap.
It's beaten, ground& cursed into preciousness

Fragment

I have a good memory, this you always tell me,
but i am only the idiot of what happens to me.

Fragment

But in the days, the months, the sleep to come,
i will speak of you with myself often.

Fragment

Who but gods could have trained them:
the mountains, those foothills, these stones,
who but titans: wind& rain, fire
&the madness a man is . . .

What bulbous chaos could shape them?
Could make them tame as footpaths
forged toward nothing certain
or a certainty only in shaping& shaping form.

Fragment

What happens will happen
like hospitals, like oceans.
I only tether my shadow,
the day bats its ball.

I don't know durability.
My craft was broken before me.
But, i know my soul doesn't travel
&not because it can't.
      It doesn't want to.

On a photograph of yr face

This image does eat yr face,
usurps it at all intersection
as if, entering a room,
i might know you now
having spoken all our past
thru a wall or blindfold or phone

&it is not fair
as thru my strangeness
i had cultivated so many affects
&by yr strangeness
you registered so many faces

&i would prefer to be wrong
in all my bygone thoughts
than lose everything
to this inflexible person.

I scoff and offend

I scoff& offend& sing wind
in the form of words to the back of my hand,
                into nothing.

Hear me, get me to a party; a circus of bodies
w/ faces flushed& fleeting, tormented
by selves made soft w/ liquid
        &fear &darkness;

to forget the cold math of heat,
to lay in yr tomb, pull the covers, to sleep;

i deceive w/ intentions the animal my want is,
take from me these phantoms
&still i'll imbibe& grope for& wail&
seek the coinage of flesh&
know what i want ### but act like it isn't.

The quick orchids my hopes is

The quick orchids my hopes is,
they flourish to their environments
&yet are fragile things, coveted;
they itch like dogs' wounds&
swim like fish or flop for breath;

they augment my consciousness
&domineer my lungs& chest w/ leaves& rocks;
they fall off for present feasts, available flesh,
a sudden instance or new reference, painful defeats;
they make days& nights unfaithful clocks
that short, lag& surge;

handfuls i have forgot: stratagems, eyes, names
&, others came& went like matchsticks, some are polestars
while more remind themselves to terrible dreams;

by hopes i've been aspens or coiled upon floors as rope is,
withered& went dormant, but sans them&
i am only stone& dumb conduit, just accidents.

LOCAL TRANSITS II

Not the falling stars of headlights

Not the falling stars of headlights on radio wires
nor prehistoric orchestra composed cricket bows
could stagger this tap water cold.
w/ two coats i can't keep the world warm
or move quick enough to direct sunlight for plant life;
butterflies, strewn reflectors, a mess of broke brown or green glass,
red. The burnt-out auto wrecks of bare autumn branches,
a catastrophe of ghostly cars on apocalyptic highways.
Yr cheek had the heat of a noon warm cat
&our hands intertwined were winter petals,
                              cold weather sepals.

Easy to forget

Easy to forget: cats' day-like soft stomachs,
honeyed teas' aftertaste,
sunlight on carpets in winter months,
the spring scents that seduce bees' mouths,
&inexplicable texture aluminum is
— such a smooth grit

from the other side i am the same but different;
leaving trails w/ movement the worm accumulates dirt
(yr sweater hung from you like an upside-down tulip
 &hair smelled of earth& bark, of moss.)

All these ordeals of hips

All these ordeals of hips, i do not eat often or right
&malaise i stable frequent. Don't talk so long, i fidget
— my eyes rift, they drift the windowpane-street
&passing trucks' neon monograms, airbrushed,
"auto glass detail" "Johnson's" "Jacob's"
&10thousand sons, a city bus. The sun is dumb&
falls unfeeling as airplanes, heart-stopped pigeons
but always& always warm when my eyes scrimp.

Once my lover'd angel-tipped

Once my lover'd angel-tipped a tree.
I stewed, curling lowly
where upturned roots soup-bowled earth,
tangled in w/; i'd known she'd flown me.

Birds stalk worms& i'm lowly,
slop up dirts in my slitherish stampede —
not nothing leaves me:

wet leaves& cut hairs, walled eyes,
— closed hard in an open glaring. Listen,
i'm sticky& there's aching. I hurt much&
curl in roots' soup-bowls. I bury me.
My lover, once, angel-tipped a tree.

And what of it

&what of it, in a high place talking to a girl of this . . .
Disinterested, but lonely still. Then touched
&didn't. Listen, i'm sunk as ships is
 — too tired for drowning.

Let me lease a single bed on some lost continent
&let me sleep, smoke& practice drawing,
let me tinker w/ botany or watch building
 — invent calendars which include
lines you sleep thru so the weeks seem to move
 — let there be days i don't think of you.

Not marble nor stained glass

Not marble nor stained glass,
not coarse nor all of a piece,
but innumerable moving parts
these breathing bodies are;

all my loves were mechanical birds
who ran on steam
&the brittle thin seed of words,
i liked the taut& firm of them,
their alloys, their dyed tins;

but what quick faith yr touch is,
what a fluid swift yr sweat.
I am all fire, a hesitant, &have no sobriety of action;
yr presence is like the night&
the thought of you like the night;
my lips no longer tremble to read these books
nor shaking do i bend before an image;

i've lost one bark as it fell to the next.

What is pretty is prey to deformity
&how, after so much failure, so much breath,
how did i not know this?
That what we see can blind us,
what coolness we touch burn us afterwards,
that uncertainty eats up houses;

&i think to myself i may pray for a dog's face,
for the strange bent haunches of a hound's legs,
                         i will pray for this
because i do not have my own strength,
because when things are less simple they wound us.

They are just phantoms

They are just phantoms,
these wisps of loins, words& glares,
a murmur of sharp exclamations:
"yes&" "yes&" the distrust, bickerings;
less than gravel, a rock i broke
                in falling forwards;

but still, it's the ground i skitter on
&the wind that resists my frame
&it's the boilers in the darkness of my reaching forth;
the swallowed dust of my sculpted speech.

Though, i have extended beyond my shape,
sutured in my recollect chimeras,
i mean a hyper-sorrow of bodies
with small nipples like açaí berries:
                round& dark& lean
&, sometimes, shuddering, this canceled me.

Often a sad wild knowledge
presses like a thick book upon my mouth
that is read in the flare& depth of my eyes,
a weight that droops my shoulders;

i will lay still with narrowing shoulders
regardless of my youth or age:
yards of zipper& notebook wire, pounds of beard,
regardless of what i ate
            or the mandalas of hairpins
unearthed in my migrations;
just headstones, anonymous samples,
as my traitor name is the example of a name;

i mean, where i went, who'll notice?
Who'll sense the new distance of my vulgarity& rage,
                    my quietness&
who'll laugh at my good friends' drunkenness
            or sing of the immutable stone
              that has all power& no throat?

When the best of me is grafted to the trees of speech
&my hair sprouts in *versts* from my enforeigned bones;
i mean, when the habits of my joints are done.

The night may change us

The night may change us, i don't care,
i'm not certain who i am;
today will be played upon me
&those others& you as well. Sometimes

i am simple& older
&no longer keep youthful track of my numbers
(my kissing having become glasses of water).

I've lost hold of what i hoped for,
happy to wake& boil water
while you sleep knowing i'm there.

What i know is that i will know less
full moons than the varied blue
of day skies in yr coffee cups,
less of rain than ways of saying yr name.

This book is set in Sabon
by The Center for Literary Publishing
at Colorado State University.

Copyediting by Denise Jarrott.
Proofreading by Sam Killmeyer.
Book design and typesetting by Zach Yanowitz.
Cover design by John McDonough.
Cover art by Crockett Bodelson.
Printing by BookMobile.